VISHNU
SPEAKS

**Messages of Enlightenment
from the Ancient Deity**

Cindy Riggs

Acknowledgments

I would like to express my deepest gratitude for all beings – spirit and human – who have encouraged and supported my psychic and spiritual growth since the mid '90s, particularly my own spirit guides who continue to teach me the most amazing and powerful techniques, such as the trance channeling that has made this book possible. It is my absolute honor to be a vessel for information that may assist the evolution of humanity. A special thanks to Alicia Adams for her unparalleled support, to Susan Rawlings for helping me launch my spiritual work, to my husband Matt for his grounding presence and unconditional love (and assistance with formatting), and to Robert Backoff for his support as well as his loving presence the moment I first encountered Vishnu.

Preface

One of the most powerful deities of Hinduism, **Vishnu** means **all-pervading**. In Vaishnavism, Vishnu is the sole or Supreme God reigning in the highest heaven. In popular Hinduism, Vishnu is known as the Preserver, the protector of the good and the guardian of Dharma, the law of righteousness and moral order. He is one of the Trimurti ("Great Trinity") with Brahma the creator, and Shiva the destroyer or transformer. Vishnu is said to have 10 incarnations, two of which were **Rama** and **Krishna** (with the tenth yet to come); and is said to repeatedly incarnate himself to put an end to unrighteousness. Vishnu's consort is **Lakshmi, the Universal Mother.** Source: *The Book of Vishnu*

Vishnu is closely identified with sacred water or *nara*, his presence pervading the Ganges. Vishnu is generally depicted with four arms, typically holding attributes such as conch, discus, prayer wheel, and a mace of authority. Around his neck may be the sacred stone, the kausrabha. Source: *Encyclopedia of Gods*

VISHNU SPEAKS
Messages of Enlightenment
from the Ancient Deity

Contents

Introduction

My journey with channeling began in 1997. I began writing down messages I was "hearing" (clairaudiently) when I was awakened repeatedly at 3:15 am. These messages quickly evolved into my ability to relay what I was "hearing", and ultimately to allow the spirits to merge with me and speak directly through me. Over the years, I grew to accommodate beings of higher and higher frequencies.

My journey with Vishnu began on April 1, 2010, as I began to channel for myself and my friend Robert in the same way that I always did – with no expectations of who might approach me that day. (Over the years, I had had some channeling experiences with a few Hindu gods, such as Shiva, Kali, Durga, Ganesha, Rama, Lakshmi and Hanuman, as well as literally thousands of other Light beings). First I saw a trident in my mind's eye. Then when I "heard" the name Vishnu, I recognized it from Hinduism, but was not sure exactly which god he was. I proceeded to channel him that day and his energy was the most intense I had experienced to date, accompanied by the color saffron and a sensation of warm water coursing through my body. Later I researched him and was astounded to discover that he was known as a "god of gods" or supreme creator god, as well as one of the trinity with Brahma and Shiva.

Vishnu suggested that I allow him to "work" with me on a daily basis, which I proceeded to do during my morning meditations, allowing him to merge with my energy fields (physical, mental, emotional & spiritual), and simply *be*

1

with him as he performed energetic repatternings for me – which he called "ascension codes" - to raise my frequency and assist me in my spiritual evolution, as well as perform healing work and the transmission of ascension codes to others in my private practice.

I have discovered that the more I let go of expectations, the more profound my experiences can be. Very little communication took place during those meditations, although a few times, Laskhmi (his consort) accompanied him and I merged with both of them, which I understood was for the purpose of balancing the masculine and feminine energies within my Self. At those times, the energy was even more intense. The merging of both Vishnu and Lakshmi has also occurred while performing energy healing work for others.

A few words Vishnu personally shared with me on April 22, 2010:
"Freedom is a concept, not a tangible."
"Spiral your Self into the center and *be*."

On July 20, 2010, Vishnu told me he was ready to begin a book, I felt my third eye center (brow chakra) open, and I proceeded to channel the following information:

"I am Vishnu, god of gods. Supreme god, masculine aspect of Creation/Creator. Grateful that you have allowed me to channel through you my information, my energies.

The purpose of this book is to re-introduce myself to the
world, to re-introduce my energy to the world. It is not
that the world needs to know who I am as much as my
introduction needs to be in the world in order for it to
directly affect the collective [human consciousness]. I
wish to share many things, many concepts, many Truths.
I wish to share wisdom and knowledge, and yet it has
already been shared numerous times in numerous ways.
And while it is not the information that is important, it is
the frequency - the energy frequency. (See Chapter Six.)

You have guessed correctly that I bring a frequency that is
similar to the one you call the Master Jesus, bringing a
frequency of the Christos into the human experience. I
have brought - and bring again - a remembrance of my
particular frequency. I brought it at the time that I was
incarnate, all of the times I was incarnate, and I bring it
now in this manner. Because it is not necessary to
incarnate again if I have a channel such as this one - you,
with which I can share this frequency. So you are a
conduit - my conduit - so that I may share my frequency
once again with the human race, with planet Earth.
Particularly at this time of intense need. I am Vishnu. I
come to you with Love and with power. Love and Light:
Love: the inspirational power; Light: the expressional
power.

Who am I? As mentioned before, I am the masculine
aspect of Creator/Creation Itself, known to the Hindu
faith...however I do carry a different frequency than the
one called Osiris. I carry a different frequency than many

of the other names of which the masculine aspect of
Creator has been known. None are better than others, just
different.

So perhaps you are thinking "why the masculine aspect at
this time, when there has been so much masculinity on
this planet in this [human] collective, and it is the
feminine that seems to be needed?" It is always both that
are needed, always both in balance. This is why later in
the book Lakshmi and I will speak together. However I
begin because your society is still patriarchal, because
your society is still focused on *doing*, because your society
is ego-driven. And while I'm not associated with ego, I
am more closely understood in a society which is still so
focused on *doing*. My message, of course, is always about
be-ing rather than doing, which shifts one's consciousness
more toward a balance, more toward the feminine at first,
and then toward the balance of both, once the feminine is
understood. You do not have time for the feminine to be
understood now. And so I have come in to try a different
angle with your human understanding, one that is
assertive, powerful, strong; and yet balanced. Power is
not always force. True power is gentle, is easy, is smooth,
and yet it takes motivation. This is why I have come - to
help to motivate the humans, the minds of the humans. I
have come to help to unlock the understanding toward
that motivation. Most humans wait for motivation to
occur, from outside sources or other influence. And yet
motivation that is directed toward a particular goal of
manifestation - be it personal or global - cannot come
from outside the Self. It must be self-motivation. It must

occur as a pointed action. This will be our first topic, Self-Motivation.

I am always present, always present with you, especially now. Thank you for integrating me on a daily basis. This has been critical in our growth and evolutionary process together, and we have been able to reach a point where we can begin this material - much sooner than I had originally expected. This is excellent, as the sooner the information can be available, the sooner it will begin to assist."

At this point, I (Cindy) became curious about how to accomplish this task.

"You are asking me how to motivate the people to obtain this book, or how to get an audience. Do not worry about this. Hindus automatically will know who I am. Others will be intrigued, ready for something new, ready for a new angle, a new message. And even though the message itself is not new, the way in which it is presented will be new.

Thank you for agreeing to move forward and see this project through to the end...which will only be the beginning. Once you are finished with something, it is always a new beginning. Know that this project can be a new beginning for the human race.

I am Vishnu, god of gods."

Because you are holding this material, you are ready for spiritual expansion of awareness, clarity of mind and truth, and you are one step further along your chosen path of evolution. You are ready to rise above third-dimensional duality, and overcome the intensity of contrast, even if you are not certain what that means yet. I can assure you that this material can profoundly affect your life as it has mine, if it is accepted with an open mind and heart.

It is my honor to share with you the words and energy frequencies of the powerful and, loving god-spirit Vishnu.

In Oneness -
Cindy Riggs

Chapter One
Self-Motivation

What do you want for yourselves? Things? Ideas? What are your driving factors? If you can look into your Self and determine some very important factors, you can quickly shift your awareness toward self-motivation., and I will show you how. If this already sounds like too much work, then realize you are operating under false pretenses. I shall explain.

For you to desire something – anything at all – there must first be a *motivating factor*, something that causes you to desire the thing. Nothing could be more important than determining the motivating factor. It is the foundation of that which you desire. It determines whether or not you build or manifest something that is long-lasting or something that is short-lived. Your society is focused on instant gratification – the "short-lived." If you desire the short-lived, then you *are* the short-lived. And when that thing's "life" is over, then you have to start all over again with a new desire. It's no wonder you are all so exhausted most of the time.

Now, let's talk more about the motivating factors. There are two ways you can think in the duality of your world: from *fear* or from *Love*. Throughout this material, I will refer to each nature in a different way, since you all have such unique concepts of that which you call love, and the conditions associated with it.

7

Fear is every thought and subsequent emotion rooted in your ego self (the part of you that is selfish, competitive, and lacking in self-confidence). Fear is at the core of every negative thought and every negative emotion. Fear is also illusion. It is not "real."

Love – or *Truth* as I will call it from this point forward – is every thought and subsequent emotion rooted in your *True Self* (the part of you that already knows that all individuals are connected as One on the highest level of your beings, and also that you are all equals in the eyes of that which created you. I am an aspect of that which created you.) Truth is not something you have to figure out or find. Truth is already there. You simply need to get your *fear self* out of its way so it can shine through you. So it can inspire you. So it can guide you. It's already there. As is all of the information and wisdom you will ever need - already there.

Whatever "but" you are thinking about right now…let go of it. Your fear self will try to find every excuse to keep you in its grasp, in its drama. Let go of it. Whatever it was about to say about who you are, what you are capable of, what you deserve, it's all illusion. It's not truth. It craves drama. Stop choosing to crave drama. You're addicted to it. A large percentage of humans are addicted to it, because your fear self's purpose is fight or flight, and in most of your modern societies, it is no longer needed, however it's still intact just in case. And because there are still some societies in which it is needed – those in remote areas of nations who still live in tribes and those in places of war and true physical danger such as poisonous snakes – it will remain intact in the human species until the entire collective reaches a point when it is no longer needed, globally. (This is no time soon.)

On the other hand, if your True Self was about to agree with the above statements, then you are already operating from it. You already understand the two parts of your Self. If you do, then this material will serve as a reminder. If not, please read on so I may assist you.

If you are *present* enough, which means that your thoughts are here right now (not in the past or the future), you can notice what is motivating every thought, emotion, decision, and desire. And it can only be from one of two places: *fear* or *Truth*.

Think of something you desire right now – anything at all. And when you think about this thing, how does this thought cause you to feel? Anxious that you may not get it? Silly because you desired it at all? Confident that you will get it? And then, what will getting it give you? You need to examine these things – each one. Dissect what motivates your desires.

If any of the following thoughts or emotions are present in your desire, be aware that it is motivated by fear, which is illusion, which is temporary, which is likely instant gratification, which is ultimately not evolving your Soul, or moving you forward very quickly:

Anger
Anxiety
Guilt
Attention from others
Appearing better than others
Success
Indecisiveness
Insecurity

So what thoughts or emotions might be present in your desire if it is motivated by Truth?

Confidence
Trust
Inner Peace

And the *knowing* that it not even *be desire,* rather simply a *request* for something to help you along your spiritual evolutionary path. And that request is *without attachment to how or when it manifests,* because you know that all you ever need is always given in the right way at the right time. What is "right?" Divine order. What is Divine order? Your own, perfect timing, governed by your True Self. Divine order can speed up if you get your fear self out of the way of your True Self.

I am not giving you these concepts to ponder and see if you choose to integrate them into your belief system. I am giving them to you so you can adopt them right away. Am I asking you to believe in me or worship me? Absolutely not. I am asking you to believe in your True Self. Do you know that you can change your beliefs in any moment? Do you also know that you are the only one judging your beliefs to determine whether or not they are Truth? Please remember that Truth is already programmed into you. Your Truth. This is how you can motivate your Self. By examining your motivating factors. When then are aligned with your True Self, you are automatically guided every day and will know what action to take. It's easy and will require little effort. So hopefully you are beginning to understand that self-motivation is more about letting go of fear than it is trying to force your Self to feel, or think, or operate, or get something first in order to feel "motivated."

Many of the concepts I will present to you will seem completely backwards of what you have always been told to be true. Get used to it. I intend to shatter your reality so that you may find your Truth…if you will allow it to shine through you.

Motivate your Self. No one and no thing outside of you can do it for you. And you do it not by *doing – by be-ing*.

Chapter Two
Right and Wrong

The next thing for you to understand is that there is no one – no human on your planet – who can tell you right from wrong. No human who can qualify *your* Soul's evolution. No minister, no doctor, no "expert." All of those things are human-based organizational systems put in place for third dimensional purposes. If you are still looking outside of your Self for validation, for acceptance, for recognition, then you are still operating from your *lower self*, I will call it. (Your "fear-based" self is more correct a term, although perhaps too harsh as I do not want you to focus on that concept in order to manifest more fear-based experiences.) Just continue to notice your motivating factors. Validation, acceptance and recognition from others are motivated by your lower self. Your True Self does not require any of these things in order to evolve your Soul. When you begin operating from your True Self more and more, you will rise above these concepts and understand that they are irrelevant.

And what of decision-making? What are the factors motivating your decisions? Are you able to even make a decision? If you have difficulty in this area, realize that it stems from a lack of self-confidence. The fear that you will make the "wrong" decision. Your True Self has already told you the best decision to make. Did you hear it? Feel it? See it? It was there – in that split second when the issue first arose. Can you remember? Or are you filled with all of the ideas your lower self has – the fearful ideas?

Right and wrong are illusions. They do not exist except as concepts in the mind of the lower self. Your True Self already knows which way to go that will serve it best *at this time*. This time – realize that *this time* is all you have. Realize that many of the issues in the past, which seemed so important at the time, are no longer important or fueling emotion. Then realize that the decision you are about to make will also feel no longer important in the future.

If issues of the past are still fueling emotion, then you have some work to do – some shifting of awareness. "Shifting of awareness" is *all* that is necessary for every situation. It is all you can control - the shifting of *your* awareness. Continuing to judge a past situation as "bad" continues to fuel your future manifestations with that quality of thought energy, which creates more "bad" situations or issues to be dealt with. Do you realize then, that you are simply fueling your lower self's desire for drama? Whether it is trying to get the attention of others (fear), or feel better about itself by comparison to others (fear), or being indecisive in order to feel the dramatic emotions (fear), it is still your lower self blocking you from moving forward.

This lower self is part of you, and you cannot eliminate it. It's part of the whole reason you came here – to awaken your Self to your dual nature and use it to your Soul's evolutionary advantage. So let's discuss *evolutionary advantage*, which some refer to as "highest good." I do not wish to use that terminology, as it is weak, and based in lower-self thinking. It has the best intentions as a blanket statement – "highest good" – yet falls short because it includes the word "good", which has programmed into it its opposite. Good is an illusion based in duality. Can you feel the difference between stating that you want your *highest good,* or that you want *that which is aligned with your Soul's evolution*?

Get out of your head. Get out of your mind. Bring your awareness into your heart center where the Truth is waiting for you to discover it. It only takes a split second to disconnect from all of the lower self's thinking and re-connect with your Truth. You may ask to be shown what is aligned with your Soul's evolution, then get your mind out of the way. You are being shown all day long, every day, in a multitude of ways in your physical body, in your intuitive awareness, in your environment, and through people, numbers, nature, music, art, and media, to name a few. Have fun with creating your reality every day by asking for that which is aligned with your Soul's evolution, then allow it to show you what that is. Perhaps it is going to your job with a different, fear-free, attitude. Perhaps it is meditating then doing your chores. Perhaps it is choosing to feel free of stress and anxiety. Perhaps it is simply making a decision you have been anxious about, because you choose to remember that you already know what to do.

Choosing...what a powerful tool you have here - choosing. I am asking you to be "pro-choice" with your Self. It is the most valuable tool you have to navigate this third dimensional/dual reality. Choosing to let go of fear about a situation. Choosing to let go of things that happened in the past so they can no longer affect you. Choosing to remember that you are a Divine Soul rather than a personality. You choose what you think about everything, and subsequently how you feel. Everything is your choice. Do not be a victim to lower mind thinking - however if you choose to be, is that "wrong"? Is it "bad?" No. However it may not be aligned with your Soul's evolution. Do you see? There is no punishment for lower mind thinking/choices, except for lower mind experiences which you manifest with those thoughts and choices. You get what you choose – [though] not literally most of the time; you get what you ask for with the vibrational frequency of your thoughts and beliefs.

So what of beliefs? What of religion? Beliefs are thoughts that you continue to choose to think each day. Religion is simply a practice of reinforcing those thoughts. So it would stand to reason that you could change those thoughts at any time, and choose to think the new ones each day (which then become beliefs), and that becomes your new religion. Think of all the things you do religiously: brush your teeth, watch television, eat meals at certain times and in certain ways, etc. What is your religion of thought, of belief? Perhaps you are thinking "but my religion is associated with going to a church or temple or mosque." If so, *and if it is contributing to your freedom of choice with thought, and if it feels as though it is contributing to that which is aligned with your Soul's evolution*, then it is appropriate. What? Were you expecting the Hindu god to try to convert you to a particular religion round about now? No, absolutely not. Religion was designed for dual-natured humans to remember who they are. It was also designed for lower minded humans to have something to believe in until they could believe in themselves – their True Selves. It was designed to give the masses guidelines for living so they would not destroy themselves. So let's see – how well has it served? From my perspective in viewing the big picture of humanity at this time, it has served in many ways. It [religion] is also dual in nature. It's True Self has inspired, empowered, and helped individual minds to make choices that were in line with their Soul's evolution. Its lower self has instilled fear. Fear that has inspired, empowered, and helped individual minds to make choice that were *not* in line with their Soul's evolution.

So is this what is meant by "sin" - making choices that are not in line with the Soul's evolution? Perhaps, although not most accurately. Sin, in my definition, is a choice that is what a human-based system teaches is "wrong." And because right and wrong are lower self/lower mind concepts, then sin serves to fuel or motivate the lower (fear based) mind. The True Self knows that right and wrong are only concepts, and that it is to be more concerned with *in line* or *not in line* with the Soul's evolution. How do you know the difference? You know. Trust that you know. *Know* that you know. And if you make choices that are not in line with your Soul's evolution, does it matter? How much does it matter? Well, it *isn't* matter, and it really doesn't matter. You will eventually reunite with the Source/Creator, so your choices – while they definitely impact your Soul's evolution, they also impact your experience in this lifetime and all of your future lifetimes. Don't allow this concept to frighten you or cause you

anxiety! Relax. Be still and *know*. Stillness and quiet are
your tickets to knowing. Remember that no one, no spirit,
no "supreme being' is judging you. Only *you* are judging
you. And I would recommend you reduce that to
"discernment" or "assessment." Return to your motivating
factors and determine if they are from your lower self or
your True Self. It's that simple.

There's more. And this is where it can become fun for you.
Fun is so important to understand. Your experience here,
while riddled with drama and challenges, was meant to be
primarily fun, enjoyable, worth the effort.

So you are going along and paying attention to your
guidance by noticing your motivating factors – whether
they come from your lower self or your True Self – and
then choosing to act or not act upon them. If you choose to
act, then you act in the way that you already *know* is
appropriate and aligned with your Soul's evolution. What
of conscious manifestation? What of desires and other
choices to make your life easier here?

Conscious manifestation, or "the law of attraction" as it is
commonly referred to, is a live, real and powerful system of
creation. It is programmed into your being, as your being
knows that it exists. Your society has done an excellent job
of helping you to forget about it. Fortunately there have
always been those who remembered and shared that
information, even when humans wouldn't listen. Due to
the large number of humans awakening at this time of your
reality, more and more are gaining this understanding.

However just as any other tool or weapon, it can be used in a number of ways. This tool, which I will refer to as "Creation Energy", is a neutral energetic force which operates inside your duality. It is an energy that responds to a vibrational frequency with the same vibrational frequency. It is like a mirror. You can look into a mirror and see your reflection, however you are still the one who chooses how to perceive that reflection. Have you noticed that each day you appear slightly different? It usually depends on how you are feeling about your Self each day. And there are even times that you look and don't see your Self at all, because your mind is focused elsewhere.

So this Creation Energy automatically responds – or mirrors – the energy it receives. Perhaps you are already either perceiving this system as magical, or you are perceiving it as dangerous or frightening. So by now you know from which place you are perceiving it (your lower self or your True Self).

VISHNU SPEAKS

Chapter Three
Thoughts Are Requests

I am Vishnu, god of gods. Would you like my perspective? Please remember that each spirit being has a slightly different perspective, just as humans do. We exist in higher planes of frequency, however as long as there are individual consciousnesses, there will be individual perspectives. This reinforces that there are very few issues in which one answer or one "truth" reigns.

It all begins with a thought. Your thought attracts energies and creates a "thought form." The thought form then travels to locate and gather similar, identical energies. (Perhaps this is confusing to you – how they may be similar and identical at the same time, however this is true.) It then brings back to you those additional energies and approaches the outskirts of your energy field. At this point, you have the opportunity to regain the energy you started with, and also to obtain the new energy as well, more energy than you started with. Seems easy, however because it is mostly an unconscious process, it becomes more difficult the more issues you have in your field which are blocking it from integrating with you.

What are you requesting with your thoughts and emotions? Every thought/emotion is a request that is matched by same energy. This is why it has been said that *every thought is a prayer, and every prayer is answered*. Are you requesting harm upon another? Are you requesting more of the same physical health situation? Are you requesting an outcome

of defeating or controlling another person? Are you
requesting material things? Are you requesting inner
peace? Are you requesting *knowing?* Are you requesting
that which is aligned with your Soul's evolution?

What blocks this process? Insecurity. Fear. Apprehension.
Too much focus on operating from your lower self, which
encompasses every thought and emotion based in fear and
insecurity, as well as every thought and emotion associated
with unresolved issues (negative memories, guilt, and un-
forgiven situations to name a few). Operating from your
lower self also includes the state of self-preservation you
may call toughness or strength, not understanding that true
strength comes from a confident inner calm and *knowing*
state of be-ing.

To unblock your Self from receiving that which you are
requesting, you must let go. You must let go of limiting
concepts, limiting beliefs. You must let go of that which
occurred in the past that you are still choosing to define
you. You must let go of the need to be "right." You must let
go of that which is not really you – the mask you wear, or
the persona you think that others expect or depend on. You
must let go of trying to please others. It is appropriate to
choose to serve others, however *there is a fine line between
service for the evolution of Soul and service for the purpose of
getting something in return.* You must sometimes let go of
that which you believe to be "reality" or "truth", because
there is always an expanded view to be experienced. There
is always more, if you will allow your Self to believe
differently. An example: "I am destined to be overweight

22

because it runs in my family." This is a limiting belief, even if it has been "true" for fifty years. If you will simply entertain the idea that something else could be true, and let go of that limiting belief, you begin to attract a different situation.

Perhaps by this point you have thought about the concept of "karma." Karma is simply this: the same energy attraction situation I have just described, except one that spans lifetimes. It is that simple. Don't try to make it more complicated, or – especially – try to figure out what your karma is and clear it. It just is, and will play out. And you knew it would, and you wanted it to. All you can do to affect it is to shift your perception around it. (This is all you can ever do about anything anyway.) Do not label it as "punishment" or "retribution" or whatever negative label you might (usually) choose. Remember you have chosen to label everything the way you have labeled it. And you own the label maker.

What are you requesting? What are you experiencing? These things match, always. So if what you are experiencing is not acceptable to you, you must be aware enough of your thoughts to understand how you are requesting it. And then use the one power that you have and change your requests moving forward. It's that simple. Now your lower self will try to find every excuse to keep you from doing this. That's its job. And it does it perfectly – just like you knew it would. Your lower self is not something to dislike. Just something to train – like a rambunctious pet.

The Creation Energy is coming back to you right now, and in every moment. How will you receive it? Perhaps you are frightened to receive that which you have recently requested while fighting with another or while wallowing in misery. Yet you can make new requests in every moment. Focus on that instead, and turn your life around faster than you ever thought possible, because those requests will be responded to also – and immediately. If you believe you have been requesting in a positive way, then work on your state of *allowing* the return on your investment, as described a moment ago. And if you are unsure of how to let go of issues and events and emotions, and fear and victim-centered beliefs, there are a multitude of practitioners – "Light workers" – out there to assist you with a myriad of techniques. All helpful.

You must remove anxiety from this process. If you are focused on - or attached to - the return on your investment, then you are missing the whole point of the exercise of conscious manifestation. You see, you have been given/blessed with this magical ability. To use it for specific or material things, you are utilizing it from your lower self, which in turn satisfies your lower self and supports your third dimensional reality. And this is perfectly fine. However because you are reading this material, it means that you are aware/awake and want more. You want to evolve your Soul. You remember that's why you came here in the first place. So if you engage this process consciously and truly trust the Creation Energy (Source) to deliver that which is aligned with your Soul's evolution, and then also trust your Self – that you will accept what you receive into your experience – you will be operating from, and receiving to, your True Self. And when you do, the third dimensional aspect of your existence will automatically be taken care of/provided for. Can you trust this process? Do you trust the Creation Energy to know what's most aligned for you? Can you trust that whatever is presented, you can accept it or handle it? Have you built up enough confidence in your Self to handle any situation or anything that presents itself, because you know that your Soul is safe and that the third dimensional reality is only illusion and very temporary?

You have been given an introduction to what you are capable of and what is possible for you in this lifetime. "Anything is possible" is your popular phrase. And this is true. Any *thing* is possible. What I am about to do is to encourage you to expand your awareness beyond *things*. Far beyond *things*. I wish to help you to rise above any *thing*.

Chapter Four
Who You Are

You are two beings at once here. How amazing is that in itself? I, Vishnu, am one being, which borrows space from this vehicle [Cindy] in order to communicate with you in this way. Just like you and every other human, she is two beings at once, a physical human animal, and a fraction of her entire Soul (of all incarnations), which I will still refer to as her "Soul." When she allows me to merge with her, *I too* then become both Soul and animal. It is as fascinating for me as it is for you, as it allows me the experience of feeling emotions and sensing all of the lower frequencies firsthand (such as other people, objects, furniture, cellular waves, etc.). And it is particularly interesting for her, as she becomes three beings at once. Actually more than that on this particular day, as Lakshmi has joined us as well.

So you are two beings: a Soul merged with a human animal, which I will refer to as "humanimal." (Does this mean that your animals do not have souls? No, it does not.)

You are quite familiar with your human body, so I will begin there. Your humanimal is powered or fueled by Life Force Energy (Chi, Prana, Ki, Ka) whose source is from Earth. You are extensions or limbs of Earth. And this Life Force Energy is all around you, emanating from all living things (just as you emanate it) and also comprises your atmosphere. Deep within your Earth is a power core, transmitting life force to all extensions of itself (plants, trees, animals, you). *Its* source of fuel? Creator itself. Now perhaps you are thinking: "I thought I was an extension of Creator?" You are that too. Your Soul is the extension or limb of Creator, powered or fueled by It. So you are two beings at once: an extension of Earth and an extension of Creator. Every particle in your environment has this two-part nature. One part Earth, one part Creator. This means that everything contains a Soul and is conscious...*and is conscious.* The blade of grass is an extension of Earth, just as you are, and it has a spiritual consciousness embedded into it fueled by Creator. Just because you have a thinking mind does not mean that you are better than the blade of grass, just different.

And then what of frequency? Every particle of matter emits a frequency. Grass and plants' frequencies increase (or raise) as they grow and occupy more space. So do you, however yours is different. Much more complicated, because you have a thinking mind and your thoughts broadcast different frequencies all of the time. You already understand that your thoughts are requests, emitting a frequency that attracts like (similar) frequency. So because of these thoughts (and emotions), your total frequency is ever changing. Negative thoughts and emotions are lower frequencies. Imagine the sunflower. If it had a thinking mind and chose negative thoughts repeatedly, it would remain in a lower frequency and stunt its growth. Fortunately, plants and trees do not have thinking minds. Their pure Souls know only one objective: growth. Your pure Soul knows only one objective: growth. Yet you complicate that process with your thoughts, beliefs, concepts, stigmas, and fears, therefore you stunt your growth – both spiritual and physical. It may not appear that you are stunting your physical growth, yet what of cell regeneration? When you experience dis-ease and illness, you are in a state of stunted physical growth. When you experience anxiety, depression and fear, you are in a state of stunted spiritual growth.

That's the whole reason you came here once again. To play in the duality of "life." To experience the challenges it presents for your growth. To figure out new ways of doing and thinking, and to balance and harmonize your two Selves. You chose this existence, because you knew it held unlimited opportunities and free will of thought. I, Vishnu, have come to remind you of this opportunity and to help you if you want more growth. I have also re-introduced my frequency to your Earth plane through this one [Cindy] in order to inject my wisdom into your atmosphere. It is not that I am forcing my influential energy onto you. I am simply introducing my energy as a resource to be utilized, or not. So I am like an untapped resource waiting to be discovered and utilized. I am a pure spiritual consciousness, or energy. This is what is meant by "God returning to save you", although that opportunity has always been available to you. There are many "gods", many aspects of consciousness available to you. One or two you may be aware of by name, many others you are not aware of. And yet we are all One, so these "many others" are just aspects of the One. It matters not which aspect you utilize, just that you utilize conscious energy (Creation Energy) that is available to you. This is what most religions are based on – this concept of a conscious energy (or spirit) available to assist you. To "save" you from lower mind thinking. Yet *it* doesn't save *you*. *You utilize it* in order to "save" your Self. And even the term "save" is incorrect. More appropriately, it is a remembrance or a reconnection with the type of Soul you already are. It is assistance with helping you to remember that you are the same as that "god." However you are also merged with the humanimal, and your thinking mind has the power to either remember the Soul or forget it by focusing elsewhere. This was the objective of all of the "saviors" throughout all of your history, to be a teacher of, and an example of that awareness. To encourage you to remember - to *re-member*. The awareness that many human teachers are teaching you right now. The awareness that many philosophers and poets throughout the ages have attempted to teach you. The awareness that all of the religions are attempting to teach you (or *were* attempting to teach you in the beginning until they became infected with lower mind thinking). And with lower mind fears, you have destroyed those teachers throughout your history, "crucified" them. Because your species was not in balance (humanimal and Soul). When you are in balance, you remember that "good" and "bad" are just concepts. You have risen above right and wrong, because you know that those concepts are lower mind thinking. And you are still honoring and allowing your body to grow too. You are honoring your "temple of God" for each of you cannot exist here without the other. You can rise above lower mind thinking, yet still honor and accept that it is part of the human experience. It just need not stunt your growth.

Chapter Five
Wake Your Self Up: Lower Self versus True Self

I, Vishnu, have come to shake things up a bit, to jump start your awareness. And more than that, I have come to encourage you to stop procrastinating. Stop waiting for someone else, or something else, or some technique or some tragic event to finally motivate you to take action. The sooner you take action, the sooner you can experience the positive feelings you so desire, and when you engage your Self in positive thoughts and emotions, your Soul is free to evolve faster. However your lower self may not believe you deserve that. Your lower self is working hard to keep you where you are. Your lower self is trying to preserve your physical life, and it is a critical part of the merged Soul/humanimal existence. However your society has given it far too much power. Like a community giving an untrustworthy leader too much power. If you could remember the totality of who you really are, you would never have allowed this to occur. You would have kept the lower self in its place, poised and waiting for its chance to help you if/when your life was truly in danger.

The humanimal evolves, and the Soul evolves, ideally together in harmony, however this has not been the case. The rise of the power of the lower self, which I will term "low-volution", comes from the fact that your third dimensional reality has created so many ways to keep your physical body secure – in developed nations, that is – that there is not as much need for daily survival. Yet because there are still native tribes and peoples who live in the wilderness who truly do have a need for survival, those minds are still influencing the human collective consciousness. In addition, as you know, there *is* still danger. You create your automobiles to be as safe as possible, yet people are still killed every day on your roads. People are still killed every day by poisonous snakes in some parts of your world. Most of all, you are creating highly uncomfortable situations for yourselves by allowing the lower self to make your choices (choices of action and choices of thought) and to dominate your personality, therefore causing dis-ease in your physical body. Some call this lower self the "devil inside", the "inner critic" or the "ego." All terminology appropriate. Remember that it is a critical part of your experience here, and also an important part of your Soul's evolution. It can either motivate you to grow and evolve, or completely shut you down with fear. Your choice.

And because it's your choice, I would like to encourage you to continuously wake your Self up. You live here with free will of thought. You want independence? You want freedom? You want joy? All of these are concepts – not tangible – yet they are labels you assign to your emotions, and those emotions feel very real. They are very "real", because, as we have already discussed, they are energetic requests, and create more of the same energy into your experience. So to "have" these things, all you need to do is exercise your free will of thought. Simple, unless your lower self is in control. It is encouraging you to request with fear-based thoughts (all negative thoughts are fear-based).

Provided for you now is a list of fear-based
thoughts/concepts/emotions in order to help you more
easily understand this concept:

Anxiety/Stress/Depression
Control
Force
Competition
Resistance
Weakness
Doubt
Guilt
Victim
Self-Pity
Judgment
Conflict/Drama
Lack
Skepticism
Intimidation
Anger
Aggressiveness
Aloofness
Insecurity
Laziness
Indecision

Remembering now that the above thoughts/concepts come
from your free will of thought, I am encouraging you to
choose differently. That is all you need to do. However you
can't choose differently unless you *wake your Self out of the
lower self's trance*, which is very easy to do. The difficult part

is remembering to do it. What techniques do you use to help your Self remember things? Write a note? Rubber band on the wrist? Reminder/indicator on your electronic device? What if you were to remind your Self every hour to wake your Self up? What is meant by this terminology is *reconnect with your True Self.*

How might you accomplish this? I realize it is not feasible to meditate every hour. What if you simply stop for a moment, close your eyes, take a few deep breaths, and focus on the area where you believe your True Self resides. I will tell you that it resides in every subatomic particle of your being, so it is in every cell of your body and is also throughout the energy fields that surround you. (Your Soul is merged with the humanimal, remember?) However if you believe that it resides in your heart center, or above your head, that is fine too. Each individual has their own unique concept of this, and all are correct. So focus on this True Self, and connect with it, merge with it, *be* it. Or perhaps you say a statement, such as "I choose to operate exclusively from my True Self." Remember that you can't just do this once a day. You must do it continuously in order to override your lower self's motivating factors.

Only you can wake your Self up. Engage it. Pull your Self out of the lower self's low-volution. I am not giving you this information because it is the "right' thing to do. I am giving you this information because, from my perspective, it is more aligned with your Soul's evolution. I would encourage you also to shift your labeled concepts of "right" and "wrong" to "helpful for my Soul's evolution" and "not helpful for my Soul's evolution."

Operating from you lower self – not helpful.
Operating from your True Self – helpful.

Your choice.

VISHNU SPEAKS

Chapter Six
Get a Grip on Your Self: Return to Frequency

When you "wake your Self up" or re-connect with it, you instantly raise your vibrational frequency. What does this mean – "frequency?" You might define frequency as the number of times something happens in a period of time – how frequent. Also, as you know, higher frequencies have more and higher waves on your measurement devices. Do you want to have more and higher waves of experience? Do you want to jump higher? Evolve faster? Then raise your frequency. You do this by engaging, or operating from your True Self. You do it by choices of positive/helpful thoughts. By now, you are aware of what types of thought or speech are helpful or not helpful for your Soul's evolution. The helpful (or positive, loving) thoughts increase your frequency. That simple. And because they request like (similar) energy, you begin to experience helpful things in your reality, such as inner guidance, new friends, and opportunities.

Can you measure this "frequency?" Yes – with the way you feel. Here are some symptoms of a higher frequency: joy, inner peace, understanding, confidence, knowing, love, and acceptance. It is a state of fearlessness. It is a feeling that everything will be OK. It is a place of knowing that everything is Divine. Nothing is bad or good, it just *is*. Do you think this is just some fantasy that I, the god, am experiencing in my spiritual plane, "but" not attainable where you are right now? It is not. It *is* attainable, if you simply choose to get a grip on your True Self. Like surfing.

You get a good wave, and you ride it. And then it dissipates. So you need to get another wave and ride it until it dissipates. You need to keep getting onto the wave to feel that rush. That sense of accomplishment and freedom. That feeling of receiving what you requested. Wonderful feelings are indicators of higher frequency; peaceful feelings are also. When you truly experience inner peace – and it *is* possible – you will want to get on that wave again and again. And the more you do, the more you raise your frequency, and attract like (similar) frequencies.

Know that the waves will dissipate. Your goal is not to get on the wave and stay there all the time. Evolution is not about being static or stagnant. It is about always growing, always moving toward new levels of understanding and confidence. Were it not for the contrast – or the lower self's motivating factors – you would not have the opportunities to rise above – or raise your frequency. Perhaps what I mean is to more *frequently* get a grip on your [True] Self.

I am giving you this information because you requested it. It is not what you "should" be doing. It is what I know will help you as you make your way through your path of existence here. So many of you are focused on whether or not you are on the "right" path. If you are able to follow the advice that I have given you, then you will know that you are on the "right" path, because it will feel aligned. If you are unable to identify your motivating factors yet, or to wake your Self up, I would encourage you to accept that you are on your path - exactly where you are "supposed" to be right now, because if you can embrace/accept that your current experience is a result of your past thoughts and emotions, and if you can now choose different thoughts and emotions in order to request a different experience in the near future, you are on your way to understanding that you are on the "right" path. You see, your blueprint or path is not your career or anything to do with the material world. It is your Soul's evolutionary growth chart, which becomes imprinted with your choices in the third dimension. It matters not what you choose to do as you move along your path. What is important is that you are allowing your Soul to evolve while you do what you do. It is your state of *be-ing* that is most important. And I have just given you the tools and understanding in order to *be*. Everyone is just on their path. Remember that "right" and "wrong" are low-volutionary labels. You are just on your path. Accept it. And make your journey through the material world more pleasant if you like. And it will automatically be more pleasant if your objective is *that which is aligned with your Soul's evolution*.

Perhaps you don't know what is aligned with your Soul's evolution. How to know? The more you wake your Self up, get a grip on your Self, you will know. Or for now, you may simply make it your prayer: thanking your guidance for showing you, guiding you toward that which is aligned with your Soul's evolution. And then trust that it will show you in the many ways that it can make you aware. Relax and stop thinking so much about it. Trust. It takes a great deal of confidence to have that kind of trust. *Choose* to have confidence, because you have the free will to choose it. Confidence is another concept that ought to become more frequent in your awareness. Get a grip on your True Self and the power you have to choose to raise your frequency – of thought and of energy.

Chapter Seven
Get an Attitude Adjustment

Imagine that you are the expert in a subject, yet no one ever asks you about it, wants your opinion, or wants you to teach them about it. How would it feel to have all of that knowledge with no way to share it or utilize it in your world? I am here to tell you that you do have "all that knowledge" – your True Self does, however most of the time, your lower self does not give it the time of day. Remember that your lower self is more focused on your humanimal existence: survival, matter, and everything associated with those issues. Your lower self is also interested in engaging with drama, gossip, and the need to be right/better/successful/important.

As I, Vishnu, am here to help you to *rise above*, it is my job to impart my wisdom so that you can re-member [with] yours. All it takes to rise above the lower self's focus and desires, is a simple attitude adjustment. I call it simple, because it is a simple choice of thought. You will decide if it is simple or difficult, and then it will be whatever you decide it is, until you choose to think about it differently. Until you choose to adjust your attitude about that too.

This is a game you can play with every aspect of your life – every event, relationship, and situation, and especially the way you think and feel about your Self. Remember that expert? Ask it for its opinion. Ask it for its guidance. Ask it to teach you things. Ask it to show you how to do things differently – easily, effortlessly. That expert is your True

Self, and you can tap into its wisdom any time you choose with a simple attitude adjustment. How to accomplish this?

Step 1: Recognize from where you are operating (lower self or True Self)

In any and every situation where you feel less than, or feel you are being treated unfairly, or if you feel bad in any of these ways: drained, unhappy, defeated, unsuccessful, stuck, blocked, depressed, hurt, lonely, grieving, or even plagued or hexed, it is your lower self's focus on reality. And for now, your True Self, the expert, takes a back seat and is asked to be quiet. It's the genius shushed and made to sit in the corner. If you can simply stop and recognize this situation, you have completed Step 1.

Step 2: Choose a new attitude

As I have already discussed, you have the power to choose your thoughts. Every emotion is a result of a thought. Your True Self can diffuse your lower self's negative emotions by introducing a new thought. However beware that your lower self, depending on how powerful you have allowed it to be in your reality, is not only addicted to drama, it is also very clever at inventing ways to trick you and arguments to make itself right. If it seems that there is no other way to think about a situation, you must know and trust that your True Self (the expert) does know another way. There is always another way.

Hopefully you are never sentenced to life in prison. However if you are, it means that you have ignored all of the signs and guidance your True Self has tried to give you over the years, and now you must face the consequences of that non-action. Yet even there, you have the opportunity to make an attitude adjustment and help to change the world from your cell. Remember that you are part of the human collective consciousness. As you change, the whole collective shifts its awareness. No matter where you are, you are contributing to the evolution of humanity and Earth. So how are you contributing today? With your victim-focused requests of thought? Or with new choices of attitude?

So what if you cannot think or fathom what to choose?

Step 3: A technique
Imagine that your True Self resides – or is anchored in - your heart center (or chakra). While the term "higher" may insinuate "above", it is actually installed within. So sitting or lying in a comfortable position, imagine this tiny spark of energy or Light deep within your heart center. Imagine that it now grows bigger and bigger into a sphere of Light that spreads out into your chest cavity, then filling your torso, and then spreading out to fill your entire body, lastly your brain. Allow it to saturate your brain and your entire skull. Then it may expand outward to surround your whole body.

Next, realize that it is a conscious being with which you can communicate, because it is. So thank it for imprinting upon your brain a new idea about the situation and imagine that Its Light is writing something in your brain, or down-loading new information. Then simply stay (*be*) in that state of integration with your True Self – as long as you can. You may even ask it for help with other issues, or for other solutions at this time regarding health, decisions, relationships, career, etc....however remember to ask for *that which is aligned with your Soul's evolution* for each issue.

This technique may take some time to accomplish the first few times, however like anything else, becomes faster and easier the more you practice. You can reach the point where it takes only a few minutes to accomplish. Do not allow your lower self to tell you that you do not have 5 minutes in your day to do this exercise. Shift your awareness to choose to make time for it. The more you practice, the more you will benefit. Perhaps it will become something you crave simply from the feeling of relaxation, peace, and doing something highly beneficial and loving for your Self.

To finish, you slowly open your eyes. Notice how you feel, and how things appear. Try to stay in this state as long as possible as you continue your day. (Or perhaps you have chosen to do this technique right before sleep. That is also appropriate and recommended. It may even help you fall asleep.)

So where is the answer? This could be the trickiest part – at first. You have the answer imprinted in your being. Now you must let go of *thinking* what it must be, and instead realizing that you *know* the answer. The answer has actually been there all along. The technique simply helps you to re-connect with it. Use this power you have – your power of imagination. Because imagination is real. Your brain does not know the difference between real and imagined. Therefore it is all real. Make a real attitude adjustment by recognizing negative thoughts/feelings and then choosing a new attitude. Merge with your True Self to gain more wisdom on a daily basis, and trust that it is given, and trust that you know what it is that is aligned with your Soul's evolution. If you don't think you know it yet, merge with your True Self more often. Focus your awareness in your heart center, where the information is stored. The heart always knows. The mind is always limited.

Chapter Eight
Rise Above Any "Thing"

First of all, you have been programmed to misuse the word "thing" – rather use it for every "thing." Objects are things. And also issues and situations are "things." You have labeled every experience in your reality into matter. You think it all "matters", yet most of it does not. It is very important for you to understand what you are observing, and then labeling into something that "matters" – and what you are actually doing, energetically, is transforming neutral energy into matter. How powerful you are! And if we dissect that process, we very easily find that you are bringing an observation into the lower self's reality (the third dimension). And then you are asking it to manifest in a certain way there. Or worse, you are trying to manipulate it, judge it, or even use it as evidence of your unhappiness. This is all by using the term "thing" as a label for that which is *other than* material objects.

It may take some time and practice to realize just how often you use this "thing" terminology. "This *thing* is happening to me", "I have *things* to do", "This *thing* is too much for me to handle", "This *thing* has changed the whole situation at work", "Everyone is afraid to talk about this *thing*", "I can't stop thinking about this *thing*", "He has a *thing* for her", "this whole *thing* is the cause of my depression", every*thing* in my life is going wrong." Once you identify the way in which you are using the label "thing", perhaps you can choose to rise above it in your thought or perception.

There is another example I may offer you. It's "but."
Anytime you are using the word "but" you are limiting or
blocking your Self, and you are anchoring the situation in
your lower self; and sometimes you are also trying to
influence others to join your reality there. "Misery loves
company" you say. And "but" is the vehicle that delivers
an issue into the lower mind. "But" typically insinuates that
you disagree with what *is*, whether it is about a situation, a
person, or your Self. Your True Self does not have a "but."
It is all accepting, all flowing, and open to change. Notice
how often you use the term "but" and where you plan to
go with the statement that follows. See if you intend to
anchor a "thing" into duality, or the lower plane.

My intention is to further help you to understand how to
rise above any "thing" (object, issue, person's negative
influence, situation, etc.).

First we begin with "object." Why would it be important to
rise above an object? When you are so attached to it that it
would devastate you if you lost it, such as a diamond ring,
family heirloom, car or house. If you are operating in your
True Self, you realize that objects, while they are matter, do
not "matter" because you can see a bigger picture of reality.

Next is the *thing* you call an "issue." "Everyone has issues"
you say. However if it is labeled repeatedly as an "issue", it
begins to become something that "matters" (it *"is you"*).
And then it is anchored into duality. It still is not
technically "matter", because it is not solid. It is still a
concept. And now that concept has the power of thought

behind it, fueling it into reality; birthing it into a new world of opportunity just like a newborn baby, where it has the opportunity to grow and be validated. When you are operating in your True Self, you may simply choose to realize that the "issue" is just a concept, and if it originated in the past, or if it seems like one that may manifest in the future, you realize that neither exist, and you bring your Self back into the present, where the "issue" can either be resolved or dismissed.

The next thing is perhaps the most common "issue": the other person. Each time you allow another's opinions, beliefs (which are also opinions), or methods of influence to negatively affect you - or control you - you anchor your awareness into duality. No other person ever, *ever* knows how *you* ought to think or behave, what "issues" you are truly holding in your awareness, or what you have chosen to experience in this lifetime. Therefore, do not allow their opinions to become "matter."

Ask your Self this question in any situation: am I operating as the humanimal or the True Self right now?

If you are starving, living on the street, and you are desperate for food, you are the humanimal. Easy to figure out. If you shift your awareness to your True Self, you trust the flow and know that food will appear if you are meant to survive. Perhaps you chose to have the experience of starving to death. Is that "bad" or "wrong?" It is neither. It is just an experience that, if it occurs, helps you along your spiritual evolutionary path in some fashion.

If you become involved in office gossip (speculation of that which is occurring not based in fact), you are still the humanimal fighting to survive in duality.

Rise above these things with your mind. It all begins with your mind. Choose your True Self for a moment, and see the issue/person/object from outer space – the place of all-knowing. The place of no fear.

Chapter Nine
Surrendering and Allowing is the Easy Way

Would you like me, Vishnu, to offer you a "magic pill"? An easy way out? What is meant by this terminology: "easy way out?" Out of what? Out of where? Out of what aspect of your experience? What is the reason that you are wishing to escape? Are you even aware of this taking place in your psyche?

First of all, we explore "way out." Humanimals have been so programmed to believe that life is difficult. That it must be a struggle. And if it is a struggle, then you receive more attention and greater rewards. And many of you do receive rewards from your struggles. Those who do not appear to be struggling are not likely to be noticed, and are more likely to be chastised or judged for being "lazy" or somehow operating wrongly.

What are these rewards then that are produced from struggle? Money? Power? Recognition? Once again, if these are your objectives, then this process is fine for you. Except while most are struggling, they are dreaming of a "way out" even more so than the hope of the rewards. You are focused on the pain. You just want it to end. Or you just go on vacation and delay the reward. You cling to life, yet the life you are clinging to is perceived as a painful one, one of hardship and sacrifice. So many labels you have given to one thing – the perceived experience of your fearful lower self.

Again, because you are reading this material, it means that you desire more than just the manifestation from your lower self. However you are thinking "I must have money to survive." I am not denying this fact. I am about to explain – in a way that I hope will be understood: **money attracted from your lower self, your lower vibrational frequency, holds that same energy within it. So it continues to attract more experiences of hardship in order to continue replenishing it. Money attracted from your True Self, your highest vibrational frequencies, holds that energy within it. So it continues to attract more experiences of effortless abundance.**

You are told that it is bad or wrong to live your life easily. The ones you judge as lazy or ignorant are perhaps the ones that ought to be your teachers. What is it about the way they operate that could teach you something? You call it good moral value to work hard for your income, and those who do not are "taking advantage" of the system in some way. Perhaps this is true. Perhaps they are taking advantage of a system. They are doing it from a place of fear. Fear that they are not good enough or smart enough or confident enough to take any kind of action in order to move themselves to a different place financially. How many in your welfare system are living large in luxury? You judge these people as lazy and yet where is your compassion for their inner struggle? Where is your compassion for the fact that they are stuck in their lower selves? They are not wrong. They are simply a more dramatic example of you. They have just temporarily given up on trying to understand the power they have, and have relinquished responsibility for themselves. They have forgotten their True Selves.

I must now remind you that struggle is a mental concept.

What of those who are born into wealth and never appear to have to struggle? Do not judge these individuals either, because many of them have their own inner struggles. Some do not. Some are receiving their reward in this incarnation. A very good reason to follow the advice I am about to present to you.

More about struggle first. Your lower self believes that you are not deserving of reward, and at the same time, it believes that you *are* deserving, based on the "dues" you have paid. And each lower self has a different definition of "dues." It is aware of the concept of karma, and yet tries to pack it all into one lifetime, because it is uncertain that other lifetimes exist. Its focus/awareness is this lifetime only. How to know what has occurred in all of your past incarnations, or what is to occur in your future incarnations? You cannot know the whole picture. You knew that coming back here, and that was one of the most attractive features of this opportunity. If you can accept that concept alone, it will help you to surrender to the flow - or frequency – to which your True Self is attuned.

You are given examples of struggle all around you – from others and also from your pets. You pet contracts a disease because it is exhausted from contributing its energy toward helping you with yours. It tries to begin its transition. Its energetic job is completing. You do what you can to make it physically comfortable, yet when to stop with the surgeries and the medicine? Its body wisdom knows when to allow its transition to take place. So while you cling to the life of your pet for your own benefit, you continue to drain its energy – even more quickly than before. This is the same as stealing from another person – energy, that is - which also happens frequently. If you love any thing or any one, you will set it free. You will allow it to operate independently. You will allow it to own its energy and contribute or share when it chooses to. The pet example is no different that attachments to other people. If you are in a marriage, you uphold an agreement of partnership, however clinging to that person is harmful to both parties. It produces struggle in a myriad of ways. If you are a caretaker of one who is immobilized, then you must always view that situation with pure Love because it is something you have chosen to do. You must also take care of your Self even more so, so that you do not drain your Self of the energy that belongs to you. This immobilized one has already chosen how to allocate its energy. Respect that choice, regardless of the struggle that appears, because the challenges are what that person chose from some part of themselves.

It is important at this point to remind you that each situation in unique. Each individual's chosen expression, chosen experience, and karma. That applies also to pets. I have used some generalizations in order to help you shift your perception. It is not the case for each person or each pet. *No absolute answer for any situation.* It is very important that you understand this concept. And it is very important for you to understand that you must let go of attempting to understand "why" in any given situation. Remember how you knew you would not be able to see the whole picture? You love mystery. Embrace the mystery in your experience here. When you watch a movie you cannot see the camera crew. You are only seeing part of the reality of the set. This is the same in your life. Accept that. Your lower self wants to figure it all out, and tells you that it's important to do so, because it is interested in being right and in control, which is impossible. What really matters? Your Soul's evolution. Your True Self knows this.

Chapter Ten
Now What?

Are you ready to take responsibility for your evolution?
Are you ready to put forth some effort in order to free your
Self from pain, accept your Self as Divine, and find the
happiness that has always been available for you to
experience? Connect with your True Self. It is very easy,
and I have already provided the technique for you. (See
Chapter Seven.)

Practice the technique as often as possible - ideally every
day or multiple times each day.

Now what?

I did not offer you a technique to help you with the do-ing
in your life, although it definitely will; I have offered you a
technique to practice *be-ing*. The more you practice be-ing:

- the sooner you will begin hearing/seeing/sensing
  messages from your True Self
- the sooner you can establish more self-control
- the sooner you will experience more self-
  confidence
- the more your lower self loosens it's control over
  your mind
- the sooner you feel happy/successful/secure
- the sooner you will understand how to easily
  manifest different outcomes
- the easier it will be for you to let go of past
  issues/patterns/behaviors

Most importantly, it will assist you in the process of learning to override duality and align your Self with your Soul's evolution (your "purpose").

If I had called the technique a "meditation", you may not have completed reading this material. That is exactly what it is, and yet it's better than a simple relaxation meditation. It's shifting the focus of your mind onto the most powerful force available to you, your True Self. And it's critical for your spiritual growth at this time in your life – especially at this time of major transformation on your planet.

Did I mention that it's free?

Chapter Eleven
Loving Reminders and Messages of Hope

Messages of hope...what can I possibly tell you that you have not heard before? And yet we have found it never hurts for it to be repeated.

Don't be hard on yourselves. This environment/this life/this reality is hard enough on you at times, particularly how you are perceiving it. Don't compound that experience by beating your Self up about something, some "mistake" you call it. It's just *a choice that did not deliver to your expectations*, that's all. Be *present* and make new choices.

Interesting that you are born into a body, very small body, with a mind erased, brand new, ready to be imprinted, and as you move through this existence you learn, and you learn, and you learn from the choices that did not deliver the expectations. And then you choose differently, or maybe you don't. Some are stuck in the pattern of choosing "badly" as you say, and that is fine too, because it feels safe to them. Anyone who continuously chooses "badly" - understand that they're only doing so because it feels safe, it feels familiar. Judgment of any kind puts you in a lower frequency. You truly will never know the entire story of any other individual. You can't see all the lifetimes, you can't see what karma is being played out, perhaps - if you have a concept of karma; you can't see why they may be choosing what they are choosing. Honor what they are choosing. And honor what you have chosen as your experience - that which you cannot change, that is; and that which you can change, do it magnificently, do it powerfully. Have greater expectations for your Self and what can be delivered for you. Have higher expectations of what you deserve. What do you deserve here? I will tell you that the Truth is that you deserve anything that you desire. And you get what you desire. ***You get delivered to you the energy that is the same frequency of the energy from where you made your request of the desire***. This has already been explained, I am just saying it a different way. This is why we go back to ***the key to all experience here: controlling your thinking, being aware of from where you are requesting, being aware of your choices of thought and subsequent emotions***. When you have control over your thoughts and emotions, you are truly empowered, you are powerful as a human being, and you are on your way to enlightenment.

Does this make sense - control over the thoughts? Because so many humans think that this is uncontrollable: thoughts, emotions, reactions. *Not* uncontrollable, *not* impossible. Most of you have a handle on that, others do not, so inspire them with your example of controlling your own thoughts [and] choosing the way you feel about situations. Help to remind them that anxiety is a choice, that depression is a choice, that guilt is a choice, indecision is a choice - isn't that interesting statement? Indecision is a choice...of fear. So you would think that *making a decision* is a choice, yes? Indecision is also a choice. Ponder this. You have already known what decision to make the moment that the options were presented to you. Questioning your Self is also a choice. Pro-choice world here!

Personalities. I wish to speak of personalities. I am supposed to be giving you messages of hope, yet I just can't help myself...or can I? I can. I'm just choosing to educate you instead, because I am the masculine aspect of Creation. And I wish to speak of personalities because sometimes personalities seem difficult to you. That is truly the only problem you will ever have here, is that you all have individual egos which are fear-based parts of you that have different concepts, different beliefs about who each individual is. Many personalities are created by fear, fear of what someone else will think, fear of "I'm not good enough", fear of "will I achieve this or will I fail?" And then the personality forms around some of those concepts of fear. (The personality is also developed from Truth, of course; the difficult aspects are created by fear.) The Truth is you are never your personality, except for when you are here. You are an eternal soul trying *like mad* to express itself through this structure of personality that is always being created. If you can remember that Soul, that pure spark of Light and Love (Truth) that you are, then perhaps

61

some of the walls can be torn away, perhaps you can experience true freedom. Freedom is a concept, yes, yet it is [also] something that you feel. It is contentment, it is inner peace, inner calm, it is the knowing that you are the internal Divine perfect Soul, perfect spirit. If you can remember this, everything else will fall into place for you. Because with that remembrance comes confidence, comes a alignment; and with alignment everything falls into place, effortlessly, naturally and in perfect timing (Divine order).

So what message of hope do I have for you? This Truth that I have already stated: that you are a Divine, perfect, eternal Spirit. Nothing can harm you, nothing can damage you, you will never die or cease to exist. You merge back into Oneness when you leave this place, Divine Oneness. However if you can merge with Divine Oneness *while* you are in this place, you shall experience magnificence (that is if you choose to perceive it that way).

Choose. Be. Love your Self. Trust your Self. Know that you know. Know that you are One with everything. Know that you are Divine. Don't just believe it, *know* it. And then see what happens.

I am Vishnu. Namasté.

Conclusion: A Summary

I have come to help to unlock the understanding of motivation. Most humans wait for motivation to occur, from outside sources or other influence. And yet motivation that is directed toward a particular goal of manifestation - be it personal or global - cannot come from outside the Self. It must be self-motivation.

There are two ways you can think in the duality of your world: from *fear* or from *Truth* (lower self or True Self).

Truth is not something you have to figure out or find. Truth is already there. Truth is already programmed into you. You simply need to get your lower self out of its way so it can shine through you. So it can inspire you. So it can guide you. It's already there. As is all of the information and wisdom you will ever need - already there.

Motivate your Self. No one and no thing outside of you can do it for you. And you do it by *not doing – by be-ing*.

Right and wrong are illusions. They do not exist except as concepts in the mind of the lower self.

If you are still looking outside of your Self for validation, for acceptance, for recognition, then you are still operating from your lower self. No human can qualify your Soul's evolution.

I do not wish to use the terminology "highest good", as it is weak, and based in lower-self thinking. It has the best intentions as a blanket statement – "highest good" – yet falls short because it includes the word "good", which has programmed into it its opposite. "Good" is an illusion based in duality. Can you feel the difference between stating that you want your *highest good,* or that you want *that which is aligned with your Soul's evolution*?

All you can control is the shifting of *your* awareness.

Here are some symptoms of a higher frequency: joy, inner peace, understanding, confidence, knowing, love, and acceptance. It is a state of fearlessness. It is a feeling that everything will be OK. It is a place of knowing that everything is Divine. Nothing is bad or good, it just *is.*

It matters not what you choose to do as you move along your path. What is important is that you are allowing your Soul to evolve while you do what you do. It is your state of *be-ing* that is most important.

The True Self knows that right and wrong are only concepts, and that it is to be more concerned with *in line* or *not in line* with the Soul's evolution. How do you know the difference? You know. Trust that you know. *Know* that you know. Stillness and quiet are your tickets to *knowing.*

Your True Self does not have a "but."

Remember that no one, no spirit, no "supreme being' is judging you. Only you are judging you. And I would recommend you reduce that to "discernment" or "assessment."

What are you requesting? What are you experiencing? These things match, always. So if what you are experiencing is not acceptable to you, you must be aware enough of your thoughts to understand how you are requesting it. And then use the one power that you have and change your requests moving forward. It's that simple.

You can make new requests in every moment. Focus on that, and turn your life around faster than you ever thought possible. You must remove anxiety from this process. If you are focused on - or attached to - the return on your investment, then you are missing the whole point of the exercise of conscious manifestation.

Stop procrastinating. Stop waiting for someone else, or something else, or some technique or some tragic event to finally motivate you to take action. The sooner you take action, the sooner you can experience the positive feelings you so desire, and when you engage your Self in positive thoughts and emotions, your Soul is free to evolve faster.

If you can embrace/accept that your current experience is a result of your past thoughts and emotions, and if you can now choose different thoughts and emotions in order to request a different experience in the near future, you are on your way to understanding that you are on the "right" path. And it will automatically be more pleasant if your objective is *that which is aligned with your Soul's evolution*.

Money attracted from your lower self, your lower vibrational frequency, holds that same energy within it. So it continues to attract more experiences of hardship in order to continue replenishing it. Money attracted from your True Self, your highest vibrational frequencies, holds that energy within it. So it continues to attract more experiences of effortless abundance.

[There is] no absolute answer for any situation. It is very important that you understand this concept. And it is very important for you to understand that you must let go of attempting to understand "why" in any given situation.

The more you practice *be-ing*:
- the sooner you will begin hearing/seeing/sensing messages from your True Self/inner guidance
- the sooner you can establish more self-control
- the sooner you will experience more self-confidence
- the more your lower self loosens it's control over your mind
- the sooner you feel happy/successful/secure
- the sooner you will understand how to easily manifest different outcomes
- the easier it will be for you to let go of past issues/patterns/behaviors

Most importantly, it will assist you in the process of learning to override duality and align your Self with your Soul's evolution (your "purpose").

You get what you desire. *You get delivered to you the energy that is the same frequency of the energy from where you made your request of the desire.*

The key to all experience here: controlling your thinking, being aware of from where you are requesting, being aware of your choices of thought and subsequent emotions. When you have control over your thoughts and emotions, you are truly empowered, you are powerful as the human being, and you are on your way to enlightenment.

You are a Divine, perfect, eternal Spirit. Nothing can harm you, nothing can damage you, you will never die or cease to exist. You merge back into Oneness when you leave this place, Divine Oneness. However if you can merge with Divine Oneness *while* you are in this place, you shall experience magnificence.

Transcript from a Special Channeling Event with Vishnu
June 8, 2010, Columbus, Ohio

I am Vishnu, god of gods. I am grateful to have this opportunity to speak to you, to be with you. My message is always to *be*. You have heard this before. Be-ing is why you are here. You are not here for doing as much as you are here for be-ing. However the doing can assist you in your be-ing, and the be-ing can assist you in your doing. So just for now, if you could *be here now* with me, all of us together - a collective consciousness that will likely never occur again. Not in this way. Very, very special, this moment. Precious, this moment that you have gifted your Self into being. And you have gifted your Self the opportunity to receive a very, very special blessing from the god of gods.

What does this mean "god of gods?" It means the highest frequency of Creative Consciousness. I am known by many names, many names. I am incarnated in all of you. Creator itself - I am an aspect of creator itself, just as you are an aspect of creator itself - just existing in a different frequency right now.

So what frequency are you be-ing right now? Do you know how to raise your frequency? I can say that by sitting in this room you are raising your frequency...but do you know how to purposefully do this? It takes only intent to raise your frequency. What does it mean to "raise your frequency" and why would you want to do this? You want to do this. All of you in this room want to do this, because you want more awareness, you want more wisdom, you want access to information that is beyond the third dimensional space. If you raise your frequency, you can access more of these things. Raising the frequency...I shall raise the frequency in the room even now - not just in the room but for all of you. You can imagine your auric field extending upward if this helps you. And another way to raise your frequency is to bring your awareness into your heart center. While I may be associated with the masculine aspect of Creation, I am very much heart-centered, Love-centered.

You have heard that Love is all there is, and this is true - All *That* Is. All there is, is everything else. You are existing in this third dimensional space and there are many other things besides Love, are there not? But you are in duality, and you knew you were coming into duality, and so embrace the contrast. Love the contrast. Express your gratitude for this contrast, because it offers you the opportunity to experience that which you experience in such a magnificent way - much more magnificent than if you were out of this body. This is why you keep coming back. This is why I keep coming back. "What a rush it is" you say when you do an extreme sport or something that is daring. That is nothing compared to the bliss that you can experience at a higher frequency, and some of you have experienced this already and do on a regular basis. And then something happens in your reality and it brings you down, back down to the old frequency. Back into the third dimensional reality, unplugging you - or - temporarily disconnecting you from the bliss. How could your focus be on anything else than being connected to bliss? And yet it is - that's how it is here. And so you as adults are re-training yourselves: re-training your mind, the way you are thinking, your habits of thought. Re-training your Self to allow thoughts to become emotion - or not when appropriate. Because your third dimensional society - or reality - has taught you to operate differently - from your dual side most often. You have heard this information before, perhaps. It never hurts to hear it again until you are a master.

I wish to express my gratitude for this one [Cindy] who has allowed me to work with her, to work through her. Some of you have already experienced the way that I can work through her, and you will all experience that this evening as you receive encoded frequencies - "ascension codes" I am calling them. You want to ascend. You want to become enlightened. This is one of the many ways that will assist you. This is not the only way. Certainly not the Hindu god being the only way for you. No, many ways. The most powerful way for you to ascend or become enlightened? Re-training your mind and consequently your emotions. Focusing on your heart center. Raising your frequency and staying there. And what does it mean to be in a higher vibrational state? It means that you move with grace and ease. That you allow things to occur rather than trying to force them. It means that you focus more on be-ing than doing. And of course there are things that you must do, however when you do them, they need not be anxiety-ridden. They need not be fast or furious. When your frequency is higher, these things become more peaceful, easier, smoother. It is also allowing your inner guidance to guide you - whatever you think that thing is...perhaps you think it is me, perhaps you think it is the other aspect of me you call "God", or another aspect of me that you call "Osiris" or many of the other aspects of me that are all the same thing. Perhaps you think it is an Angel or a spirit guide and that is fine. It makes no difference what you think it is, and no one else can confirm that for you, nor should they. *You* decide what your inner guidance is, and listen to it. It does not speak to you in words, necessarily, it speaks to you in feeling. If you are not be-ing, you are not feeling - not as clearly as you could be.

What else does it mean to live in a higher frequency? It means that you need not worry about things anymore. When you are be-ing, your mind is not in the past or the future, it is in *now*, and therefore you eliminate anxiety from your life. Perhaps this sounds like a tall order. If it does, then examine *that* belief or thought, because anything is possible and anything can be easy if you believe that it can. Your beliefs govern every move you make. Do you realize this? Think about this: what you believe about your Self and what you are capable of or not, what you believe about others and what they are capable of or not, expectations of others, all of these things are beliefs. Beliefs are temporary programs. So many humans say "this is how I am", "well, I've always believed this way." What they are saying is not what you hear. What they are saying is "I choose to continue believing this way, I choose to continue thinking this way. It is obviously limiting me - or - getting me out of doing something I don't feel like doing - or -

getting me out of responsibility." What are you really saying when you say "this is how I believe" or "this is who I am - or how I am?" This one [Cindy] was not born a Hindu and yet she has an intimate relationship with a Hindu god now. This would not happen if she had a belief that this was not possible, or that she is not Hindu...she is still not Hindu; she is open and accommodating to everything, always working to keep her mind open. And this is why she keeps having such a wide variety of experiences. And you can too. Imagine a limitless life, complete freedom. Freedom is a concept, not a tangible. I have said this before, but I want this to apply to you - I want *you* to apply this to you. Freedom begins with your mind. It is not something given to you because you live in a certain country - no. Some who live in countries that are not considered free are some of the freest minds you would ever meet, accepting and accommodating of everyone and everything. This you call acceptance, choosing harmony in every situation - harmony of thought. You call this "win-win" in your business world - "going for a win-win." How can both parties win? How can everyone win? When you are accepting everyone for who they are, everyone wins, because everyone is right about who they are...even though "right" is also a concept.

So you understand *be-ing*? You understand acceptance? Harmony? Raising your frequency? If you are wondering if you are understanding it appropriately, just decide that you are.

In your third dimensional reality, yes, there are always

humans that will be more intelligent than you are and less intelligent than you are. This is the case for everything. So, do not allow humans to label you or to tell you that you are OK or to tell you that you are right. They may not be right. They don't know what's right for you. Only you know what's right for you. I am suggesting tonight that being more open and accepting will offer you more "rights", more freedom.

I come to offer you ascension codes as I have mentioned. What will this do for you? How will this affect you? What can you expect? Everyone is unique, and so I cannot answer that with one answer, however if you allow this energy to populate your being physically, mentally, emotionally, spiritually - and it will do so in the amount of time that is appropriate for you, so you need not worry about being overwhelmed, although you may sense that it is very powerful; if you allow it to populate your being, then there can only be positive results. There can only be positive side effects. However you must *believe* that it will assist you in your ascension. You must believe that it will assist you to raise your frequency so that you can hear more of your inner guidance, so that you can sense more in your environment, so you can notice more synchronicities, so perhaps you can even become psychic, as you call it - although all of you have all of these abilities already; it's just merely about re-awakening these abilities. And there is always more awakening that can occur. So when you believe you have achieved an awakening of some kind, guess what? There is always more that you can achieve, always more - no matter who you are or where you are on your path. So many humans wonder on a daily basis if they are on the "right" path. If you were not on the right path, I am pretty sure that you would know. Only you can decide if it is the "right" path. And you have decided before you even incarnated into this body, so you will know. You would not be in this room if you were not on the right path - or - the correct chosen path - your chosen path.

Any questions for me about anything at all? You have no questions? That is a good sign. *You will know you have become enlightened when you have no more questions*, because you will become completely accepting, and you will be completely in the flow of your guidance and in the state of be-ing that I speak of all the time. Then what? There will still be contrast, do not worry. You will still have challenges/contrast while you are in this body, that is. And that contrast - those challenges - become much and much more vague. They fade away. They do not seem as dramatic as before. And you will amaze your Self when you are in a situation and you say "wow, how did I handle that so well? It just didn't seem to affect me like it used to." That's when you know you're moving even further forward on the path. But if this is not happening, do not feel as though you have failed. Failure is a concept, and I would recommend that you do not choose it as a thought or especially a belief about your Self. Failure is not a truth - not ever. Anxiety is not a truth. Depression is not a truth., Guilt is not a truth - not ever. There is one Truth, and that is Love. Not your romantic love, your spiritual Love - the connection that you have with every other human being, every other living thing, every blade of grass...everything and nothing. At its core - at its subatomic core - is vibrating Love. So you can dress it up however you like - and you have spent your whole lifetimes doing this - putting masks on it, different outfits on it, walls around it (or armor), and that is fine, your choice. It's not wrong. Just know that at your core, there it is. Not just in your heart center; in the center of every subatomic particle that you are...is Love. How could you possibly need to find it outside of you? The love that you find in a romantic way is magnificent, yes. Cannot compare to the Love that is at your core. Cannot compare to the Love that is available to you when you raise your frequency and you connect with it: you connect with your Creator, you connect with your Earth - the consciousness of your Earth or the core of your Earth - and then you connect with the core of all of your subatomic particles of your being. Or, you could just connect with all of your subatomic particles and be done with it; and yet you're connected with everything else, so it is impossible to do just one without the others. That would be like jumping into a pool and saying "I want to capture only that molecule of water over there." You jump into the pool and you are connected with all of the molecules - you have no choice. And they are aware of you. They have a consciousness, all of these molecules of water. And remember these molecules of water. You are familiar with molecules of emotion, how water is affected by your thoughts and your beliefs? You can bless your own drinking water every single day, if you just think about Love, or Light, or happiness, or joy, harmony, acceptance, all of these things - or one at a time, whatever you like. Just as you are affected when someone around you is violent or angry, water is affected by that as well. Most things are affected - most living things.

Focus on your heart center now as I prepare you for accepting the energy that I will transmit to you. This is as though I am injecting a[n energy] booster into your heart, perhaps, and yet as it is injected, it spreads throughout your body: your physical body, your mental body, your emotional body, your spiritual body, your etheric body, your ketheric body...all of the bodies and all of the multi-dimensions of those bodies that you are. Such magnificent prisms walking around, all of you - multifaceted prisms of Light and Love. Don't forget this. Don't worry what other people will think if they find out that you believe that you are magnificent, because perhaps one day they will find out that they are too, they will *choose to believe* that too. And if you choose to believe it first, they may do so as well by your example.

This is a very powerful transmission that you will receive tonight. The most powerful that this channel [Cindy] has ever been able to transmit through her. Very important that you focus on be-ing right now...be-ing here now.

(Vishnu then transmitted "ascension codes" to each participant individually. This book allows the reader the opportunity to receive the energy as well, by intending for it and *allowing* it.)

My hope is that you have experienced a moment of bliss. And if not, it is yet to come. Not just as a result of this transmission, but as a result of you choosing to allow it, to *be*.

I, Vishnu, am greatly honored to have had the opportunity to transmit to you directly these codes for your ascension, these new frequencies for you to integrate in the amount of time that is appropriate for you - at your pace - perfectly, Divinely. Your pace is Divine - trust that, know that. And your pace can be hastened if you open your Self up, if you allow more into your experience, if you are more accepting of others and of new experiences. This is how you help your Self the most. And when you help your Self, you help all of humanity. And you did not do that by *doing* very much at all; you did it by *be-ing*.

Thank you. Namasté.

About The Author

Cindy Riggs is an internationally known trance channel, psychic, spiritual consultant, educator and public speaker. She is a former producer/writer/host of a television show and has appeared as a guest on numerous radio shows. She has also written articles and audio programs.

Cindy has been channeling since 1997, which is the process of exclusively allowing high-level Light beings to temporarily inhabit her body and energy fields in order to speak through her. Much of her skill and awareness she learned from her own spirit guides. Cindy regularly channels for groups and events, and has channeled live on television and the internet. Transcripts from some of these events are available on www.CindyRiggs.com.

In her private practice, Cindy performs psychic/spiritual guidance, hypnosis, Defragmenting (soul retrieval), past-life regression, spirit releasement, energy healing, and personal & psychic development coaching. She is also a Reiki Master/Teacher and Licensed Minister.

Visit Cindy at www.CindyRiggs.com.

Made in the USA
Middletown, DE
07 November 2023

42131091R00050